Kilkenny Castle

VISITOR'S GUIDE

BY JANE FENLON

OPW

The Office of Public Works
Oifig na nOibreacha Poiblí

D1376820

KILKENNY CASTLE - A VISITOR'S GUIDE
First published in 2007 by
The Office of Public Works, 51 St. Stephen's Green, Dublin 2

OPW
The Office of Public Works
Oifig na nOibreacha Poiblí

ISBN 0755775732

Author: Jane Fenlon
Design: David Hayes
Printing: Vision Print

Acknowledgments:
The Office of Public Works, Historic Properties Division and the author would like to thank the following for their assistance in the preparation of this guidebook: Grace Marshall, Dolores Gaffney, Izabel Pennec-Murphy and other members of staff at Kilkenny Castle; Tony Roche, Conleth Manning and Freddie O'Dwyer of the Department of the Environment, Heritage, and Local Government; Eleanor Flegg for editing and copy-editing; Dan Tietzsch-Tyler; David Griffin and other members of staff at the Irish Architectural Archive; Aighleann O Shaughnessy of Historic Properties; Michael Comyns of the Office of the Chief Herald of Ireland; Paddy Friel; Marie Feeley, NGI; the Knight of Glin; Philip Mould London; Donal Fenlon, Royal Society of Antiquaries; Sara Smyth, NLI; Charles Benson, Early Printed Books, TCD.

All illustrations, unless otherwise stated, from the Photographic Unit Dept of the Environment, Heritage, and Local Government.
Photographic credits
(pages 5, 35) Royal Society of Antiquaries of Ireland, (pages 6, 9, 13) Irish Architectural Archive, (pages 12, 21, 24, 27, 28, 30, 33, 45) National Gallery of Ireland, (page 36) the Knight of Glin, (end papers and page 33) the Board of Trinity College Dublin, (page 31) Philip Mould Historical Portraits, London.

Sources
Principal sources used were documents, letters and deeds from the Ormonde family papers contained mainly in the *Ormonde Mss, Calendar of the Manuscripts of the Marquess of Ormonde* (HMC 11 vols, London), the Ormond Deeds (IMC., 6 vols, Dublin) and the collection of Ormonde Mss in the National Library of Ireland. The published work of Ben Murtagh was consulted in *Excavations* 1991, 1992, 1997, 1999, 'The Kilkenny Castle archaeological project, 1990-1993, Interim Report', *Old Kilkenny Review* 4 (5) and 'Kilkenny Castle', *Medieval Archaeology*. Other published sources used were Freddie O'Dwyer, *The Architecture of Deane and Woodward*, John Bradley, *Kilkenny, Irish Historic Towns Atlas* No. 10, James George Robertson, editor Mrs Margaret Phelan, *Antiquities and scenery of the County of Kilkenny*, archives at Kilkenny Castle in the keeping of Dolores Gaffney, earlier guidebooks of Kilkenny Castle, written by Henry Wheeler, Mrs. K. M. Lanigan and various commentaries by travellers to Kilkenny during the seventeenth, eighteenth and nineteenth centuries that are too numerous to mention here.

CONTENTS

PART I — A TOUR OF THE CASTLE

An annotated tour of Kilkenny Castle, beginning at the entrance gateway to the courtyard, this is designed to complement the official guided tour. The guidebook follows the tour, room by room, providing additional insights to the architecture, decoration, furnishings, and paintings of the castle. It also covers intriguing medieval spaces and features beneath the ground floor of the present building, which are not included in the official guided tour.

PART II — THE BUILDING OF THE CASTLE

A history of the castle, which has undergone many building and re-building programmes in the 800 years since it was first constructed. These changes are liberally illustrated with a historical reconstruction drawing of the early stone castle, plans, architectural drawings, topographical drawings. The history includes the comments of many travellers, some dating back to the seventeenth century.

PART III — LORDS OF THE CASTLE

The Marshal family — builders of the first stone castle;
The Walter/Butler family;
A family tree of the Butler/Ormond family, prefaced by a summary of their origins and with illustrated portraits of some of the most famous and colourful members of that family.

Kilkenny castle stands dramatically on on a strategic height that commands a crossing on the River Nore and dominates the 'High Town' of Kilkenny City. Over the eight centuries of its existence, many additions and alterations have been made to the fabric of the building, making Kilkenny Castle today a complex structure of various architectural styles.

The original Anglo-Norman stone castle was built for William Marshal, 4th Earl of Pembroke (c.1146-1219) during the first decade of the thirteenth century. Kilkenny Castle later became the principal Irish residence of the powerful Butler family for almost 600 years. The Butler ownership began when James (c.1360-1405), 3rd Earl of Ormond, purchased the castle in c.1391, and lasted until 1967 when Arthur, 6th Marquess of Ormonde (1893-1971), presented it to the people of Kilkenny in return for a token payment of £50.

The buildings have been in the care of the Office of Public Works since 1969, and many important programmes of archaeological excavation, conservation, and restoration have been carried out there.

The Drawing Room

The West Tower

The Bedroom Corridor

The Picture Gallery

The Parade Tower Conference Centre

PART I

A TOUR OF THE CASTLE

The Castle Gateway

TODAY THE PRINCIPAL entrance to Kilkenny Castle is through the impressive Classical gateway situated on the Parade. Before entering the archway, look to the right to see remains of the recently excavated dry ditch or moat, which was filled in during the seventeenth century to enable the construction of this gateway in the curtain wall. Also notice the heavy sloping batter of the walls, the *garderobe* chute and the small thirteenth-century Postern Gate with stone steps leading into the moat. Two circular towers may be seen to either end of the wall. The massive Parade Tower, the largest of the three remaining tower, retains much of its original proportions and fabric, although the windows in these towers are later insertions.

The massive pedimented gateway based on the classical triumphal arch dates from the end of the seventeenth century. It was largely completed before 1710 and while the finely carved Corinthian capitals and a keystone executed in the lighter coloured stone are mostly original, the decorative festoons were added during the nineteenth century. Tall wooden doors guard the entranceway and the colourful coat of arms is that of the Butler/Ormonde family. When the castle was used as a residence, a porter or gatekeeper was employed to be on duty at all times and would probably have lived in small rooms within the gateway. The gateway range has been recently refurbished as part of the Parade Tower Conference Centre.

The thirteenth century postern gate that opens into the moat.

The Medieval Room

There is a medieval room in the base of the Parade (South) Tower, which may be accessed when not in use. Features in the room include plunging arrow loops inserted in the massive walls that are indicative of the strongly defensive nature of the early castle. In the centre of the room is a stone pillar and re-used timbers dating from the later medieval period. During the nineteenth-century remodelling of the castle the room was converted to use as a wine cellar.

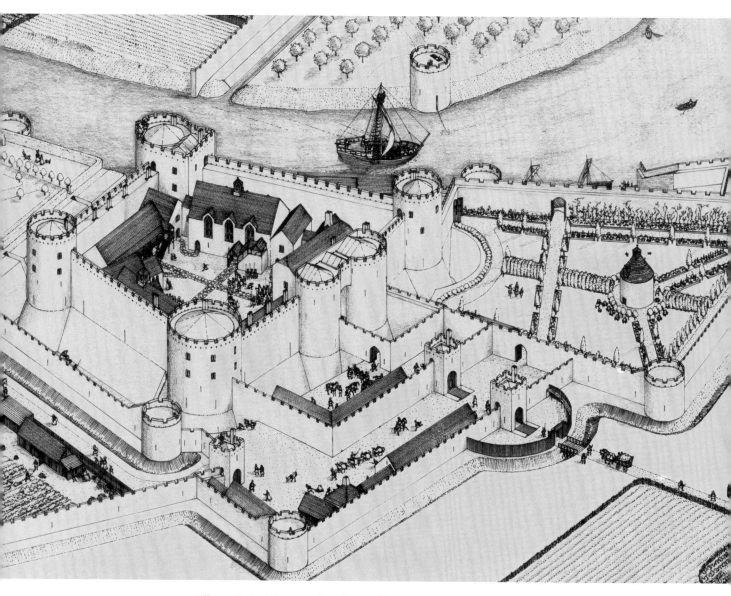

Kilkenny Castle: A Reconstruction of its Possible Appearance in about 1395 by Daniel Tietzsch-Tyler.

During a prolonged visit to Ireland in 1394-1395, King Richard II of England spent the month of April 1395 in the Earl of Ormond's great castle at Kilkenny. The reconstruction drawing attempts to show what the castle might have looked like during his visit, when it was at the height of its medieval development and before the many post-medieval changes.

The Courtyard

Entering the courtyard, the principal residential block of the castle is on the left. This was largely rebuilt in the 1830s, and the interiors were reconstructed during the most recent restoration programme. A mainly nineteenth-century range directly opposite the entrance gateway houses the Picture Gallery, its position marked by four handsome oriel windows with stone tracery and diamond-paned glass. This range was built on the foundations of a building constructed for the second Duke of Ormonde. Around the courtyard, drainpipes with elaborate, lead rainwater heads are inscribed with the date 1682 and decorated with the Ormond crest. Some of these are replicas after the original.

The rainwater heads showing the Ormond falcon rising from plumes and a ducal coronet may be seen at the top of the drainpipes in the courtyard.

The Entrance Corridor

Admission to the castle is through the central doorway of the residential block. Here a spacious entrance corridor constructed during the nineteenth-century rebuilding runs the full length of the block. Initially the central section formed a *porte-cochère*, a projecting porch for carriages, but this was later extended to encompass the largely glazed corridor that adds a Gothicised dimension to the interior and allows for easier circulation on this level.

The Picture Gallery range.

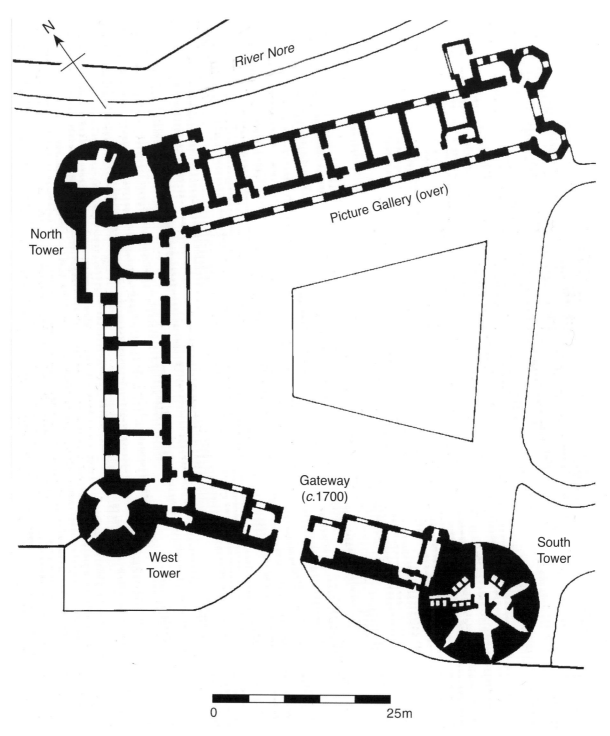

A modern ground plan of the castle.

The ground plan

The ground plan shows the current plan of the castle. The residential block is situated between the north and west towers with the Picture Gallery wing to the east and the Parade Wing to the west. The modern Conference Centre is in the South Tower. Those areas with the thickest walls are the medieval foundations of the castle.

The Undercroft of the West Tower

Although the basement is not included in the official tour, it is possible to gain entrance to the undercroft of the West Tower via a short flight of stone steps leading down from the entrance corridor. Here in a well-preserved circular chamber the massive girth of the thirteenth-century walls is evident. There are plunging arrow loops within the wall embrasures, and an example of wicker centering on the ceiling that was used to support the vault during that building process.

An arrow loop in the undercroft of the West Tower.

The Terrace Corridor

Leaving the West Tower, a short flight of steps joins a corridor situated under the garden terrace. On the right hand, a passageway that has been cut through the north curtain wall of the castle leads into a small cellar. The curved shape of the adjoining tower may be seen where it projects into the room. Excavations have revealed the footings (foundation) of a sixteenth-century building that was probably built for Thomas, 10th Earl of Ormond, before 1580. Out in the corridor, near the entrance to the cellar, a glass panel inserted in the floor covers access to another postern gate that opened into the dry moat, which ran around three sides of the castle. Proceeding along the corridor, a flight of steps at the opposite end leads back to the Entrance Corridor.

The Courtyard at Kilkenny Castle, c. 1814, showing the buildings as they were before William Robertson's remodelling of the castle.
(Royal Society of Antiquaries of Ireland)

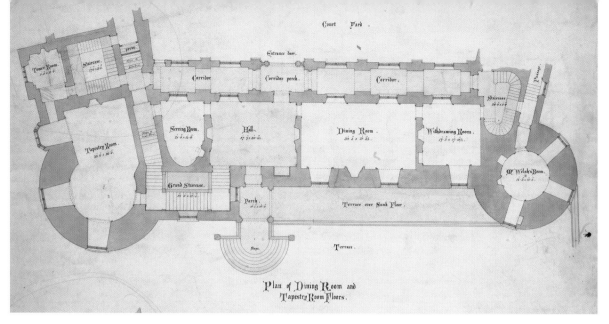

A nineteenth-century plan of the ground floor showing the arrangement and names of the rooms c. 1860 from a survey carried out by the architectural firm of Deane and Woodward. (Irish Architectural Archive)

The Chinese hand painted wallpaper in the Withdrawing Room in its complete state.

Throughout the lifetime of the castle the names and functions of rooms were altered as fashions changed. For instance, during the seventeenth century the ducal apartments were situated in this area of the ground floor.

The Withdrawing Room

This elegant room has been recreated to its original 1830s proportions. It was designated as a withdrawing room during the 1850s. Here the ladies withdrew from the dining room leaving the men to enjoy their port and cigars. Remnants of hand painted Chinese wallpaper may be seen on the walls; the monochrome infill has been carefully carried out at the studio of David Skinner. The elegant fireplace is a nineteenth-century reproduction of an earlier French design.

The Dining Room, now Audio Visual Room

The earlier Dining Room, which is now the Audio Visual Room, marks the beginning of the guided tour. This room was designated as a dining room in the 1860s. On the walls is a handsome hand blocked wallpaper. The cast iron fireback probably depicts Bacchus in his chariot being drawn by two tigers or leopards, surrounded by floral and Classical motifs.

Entrance Hall

An entrance hall has been situated here since the seventeenth-century rebuilding of the castle, although the modern hall occupies a larger area than the earlier one. The doorway cut through the massive curtain wall was twice remodelled in the nineteenth century and leads out onto a stone terrace above the Rose Garden. Features in the room include a handsome black and white stone floor that was inserted during the nineteenth-century rebuilding. Two fine marble fireplaces with heavy bolection moulding, usually a seventeenth-century feature, are situated at either end of the hall. The marble table is supported on an eighteenth-century base. Portraits include those of Thomas Butler (1531-1614), 10th Earl of Ormond, King Charles II of England (1630-1685), James Arthur Norman Butler (1893-1971), 6th Marquess of Ormonde, and Queen Henrietta Maria of England (1609-69).

The cast iron fireback, probably depicting 'A Triumph of Bacchus', in a chariot being drawn by two tigers or leopards.

The Entrance Hall.

The Grand Staircase.

The Grand Staircase

The impressive nineteenth-century mahogany staircase was designed and made by the local firm of R. Furniss and Son, the Parade, Kilkenny. It leads up to the doorway of the Tapestry Room in the North Tower; where it then turns to give access to the first floor. The painting on the stair landing is of *The Mystic Marriage of Saint Catherine*, after the original by Antonio Correggio (1494-1534) now in the Louvre, Paris.

The Tapestry Room

This large room is situated in the North Tower; here it is also possible to appreciate the massive thickness of the original walls.

The shape of this room has been altered by being opened out, although the circular section occupies the same space as the seventeenth-century Great Chamber. During that period the room had embossed and gilded leather hangings on the walls. These were replaced in the eighteenth century by a suite

A portrait of James Butler, 1st Duke of Ormond (1610-1688), by Sir Peter Lely.

of tapestries telling *The story of Decius Mus*. The Gothic-style hand blocked wallpaper is modern. Probably the finest portrait of *James Butler, 12th Earl and 1st Duke of Ormond*, may be seen hanging above the fireplace. This is an autograph portrait by Sir Peter Lely (1618-80), court painter to Charles II, and shows the duke wearing robes of the Order of the Garter holding the wand of Lord Steward in his right hand.

One of a suite of Brussels tapestries telling The story of Decius Mus *c. 1630, attributed to the workshop of Jan Raes after designs by Peter Paul Rubens.*

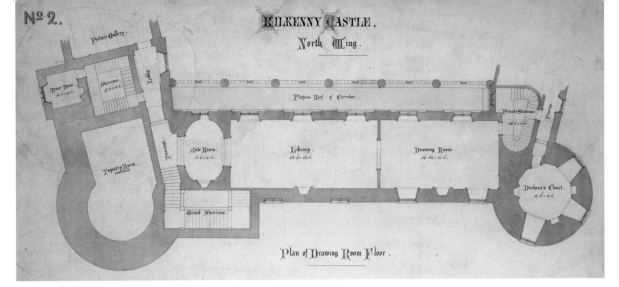

A plan of the first floor showing the arrangement and names of the rooms c. 1860 from a survey carried out by the architectural firm of Deane and Woodward. (Irish Architectural Archive)

THE FIRST FLOOR

THE STATE ROOMS OF THE sixteenth and seventeenth century were situated on this floor. At that time there was a lavishly furnished drawing room hung with a set of fine tapestries, *The Story of Diogenes*. From this room double doors led into a state bedroom and, beyond, to the duchess' closet, which was situated in the West Tower. Within the damask hung closet there was an interesting collection of small cabinet pictures. Today the space is occupied by the Anteroom, Library, and Drawing Room, as it was in the late nineteenth century.

Anteroom
This small chamber and the room below were constructed in the area where an earlier stone staircase was situated.

Looking from the Anteroom through the Library to the Drawing Room.

The Library.

The Library

The decoration of this room is a recreation of the furnishing styles of the mid to late nineteenth century when major renovations of the castle interiors were carried out. Rich fabrics are used throughout to recreate opulent, period interiors where the walls are covered in specially woven French silk poplin, as revealed by a remnant found behind a skirting board, based on the original pattern made by the famous firm of Prelle of Lyons. Garnet-red curtains of heavy quality silk damask in a pomegranate pattern made by the same firm are hung below original and matching reproduction pelmets, all gilded in gold leaf. An original glazed bookcase in mahogany stands in the corner; from this others have been carefully reproduced in the same fine wood. A large mirror over the mantelpiece has also been carefully restored and re-gilded. The Berber-style floor carpets are based on patterns adapted from Izmir motifs and these were specially woven by the firm of Woodward Grosvenor who had produced the originals.

Some of the paintings in the room are from the Ormonde collections but a number of appropriate portraits were bought in recently to replace those that were sold from the castle during the 1935 sale. Of special note are two fine small oval portraits of members of the Molesworth family to either side of the fireplace. These are executed in pastel chalks by the eighteenth-century Irish artist and master of this particular medium, Hugh Douglas Hamilton (1739-1809).

The Drawing Room

This room has been furnished in the same period style as the Library. Some surviving paintings from the original Ormonde collection are also hanging here. On the west wall is *The Five Eldest Children of Charles I*, dating from the seventeenth century, by an unknown artist after the original by the Flemish painter, Sir Anthony van Dyck (1599-1641). Among other paintings in this room are an interesting, if damaged, subject picture *An Allegory of Avarice*, signed by the Flemish painter Jan de Herdt (fl.1646-72) and several eighteenth-century Italianate landscapes. Over the fireplace are two nineteenth-century Scottish landscapes painted by a member of the Nasmyth family of Edinburgh.

The Drawing Room.

The Private Stairs, this name was applied to the secondary staircase between the first and second floors.

The Private Stairs

This staircase, which has earlier decorative plasterwork that was taken from the south tower on the ceiling above, dates from the 1830s rebuilding. Constructed of granite, from the top landing the staircase, situated in the North Tower, leads into the bedroom corridor of the same period.

The Library, looking west, as it appeared at the end of the nineteenth-century. (National Gallery of Ireland)

The Library, looking east, as it appeared at the end of the nineteenth-century. (National Gallery of Ireland)

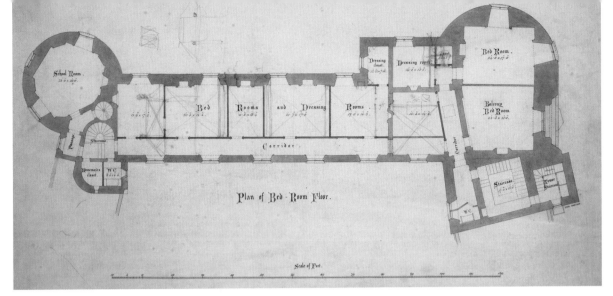

A plan of the second floor showing the arrangement and names of the rooms c. 1860 from a survey carried out by the architectural firm of Deane and Woodward. (Irish Architectural Archive)

A TOUR OF THE CASTLE

THE ORIGINAL SIXTEENTH-CENTURY Long Gallery was situated at this level, now occupied by the Blue Corridor and bedrooms. During the seventeenth century the Ormonde collection of paintings was the largest in the country. It contained paintings by Dutch and Italian masters and portraits by artists such as Sir Anthony Van Dyck, Sir Peter Lely, and others.

The Bedroom Corridor.

The Bedroom Corridor (The Blue Corridor)

This is a nineteenth-century space created during the remodelling of the central block, which allowed for easier access to bedrooms and dressing rooms along the corridor. There were three water closets situated on this floor during the 1850s. The Gothic style light fittings along the corridor were salvaged from St. Andrew's Church in Dublin.

13

The Blue Bedroom.

The Bedroom (The Blue Bedroom)

Situated in the River Tower, the Blue Bedroom is now named after the colour of the elegant wallpaper, a design by William Morris. The close proximity of the bathroom to these rooms would have been an early example of an en suite. A charming portrait of the Stanley sisters, nieces of the second duke of Ormonde by an unknown artist, hangs on the wall.

The Balcony Bedroom (The Chinese Bedroom)

This room is decorated with a modern reproduction of a hand-painted Chinese wallpaper; this *Chinoiserie* theme is continued in the oriental screen and lacquered cabinet.

The Balcony Bedroom (The Chinese Bedroom).

The Staircase

The staircase based on 'Moorish' design, offers an exciting and innovative space. It was created by the architects Deane and Woodward to allow appropriate access to the Picture Gallery and also to provide another major staircase in the circulation of the awkwardly shaped building. It is a rising half-turn stairs around a square sky-lit well with a winter garden at the bottom. Charles William Harrison (1835-1903), the stone carver, is credited with the carved naturalistic foliage and small animal details that decorate the stairs.

The Staircase.

The Picture Gallery.

The Picture Gallery Wing

The Picture Gallery Wing was built during the early nineteenth-century building programme carried out by the architect William Robertson. It was constructed on earlier foundations. Robertson's Picture Gallery, in keeping with his work on the rest of the castle, was in Castellated Baronial style. Initially the gallery was built with a flat roof that had begun to cause problems shortly after its completion. The distinguished architectural firm of Deane and Woodward was called in during the 1860s to make changes to the overall design of the Picture Gallery block, and other corrections to Robertson's work. These changes

The Picture Gallery.

A portrait of Susan Frances Elizabeth (Anne) Wandesforde, Countess of Ormond (1754-1830), by Hugh Douglas Hamilton.

included the insertion of four oriels in the west wall and the blocking up of the eight existing windows, while another oriel added to the east wall. A pitched roof was put in place, with central glazing. The hammer-beam roof structure is supported on carved stone corbels also by Harrison, It was decorated by John Hungerford Pollen (1820-1902), then Professor of Fine Arts at Newman College, Dublin, using a combination of motifs ranging from the quasi-medieval to the pre-Raphaelite, with interlace, gilded animal and bird heads on the cross beams. This decorative scheme was criticised by a contemporary, writing in *The Irish Builder*, as 'a roof probably intended to be Byzantine but is merely bizarre'.

  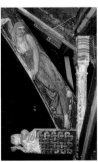 

Details from the painted ceiling of the Picture Gallery.

The Marble Fireplace

The massive double fireplace made of Carrara marble, designed by J. H. Pollen, is also in a quasi-medieval style, and was supplied by the firm of Ballyntyne, of Dorset Street, Dublin. Elegant foliage carving attributed to Charles Harrison covers the hood and a frieze beneath is decorated with the Butler/Ormonde arms and significant episodes from the family history. These depict: 'the purchase of Kilkenny castle by the earl of Ormond in 1391'; 'the chief butler offering the first cup of wine to the newly crowned king'; 'King Richard II who was godfather to the third earl's son and who visited Kilkenny castle in 1395'; 'the coat of arms of the Butler/Ormond family'; 'James, 1st Duke of Ormond, refusing to surrender his sword on entering the Irish House of Lords in 1634'; 'A Lady from the Ormonde family dispensing food to the poor'; and 'James, 1st Duke of Ormond returns in triumph to Dublin in 1662'.

Details from the fireplace showing 'the purchase of Kilkenny Castle by the Earl of Ormond in 1391' & 'the Chief Butler offering the first cup of wine to the newly crowned king'.

The Carrara marble fireplace in the Picture Gallery.

The Picture Gallery as it appeared at the end of the nineteenth century. (National Gallery of Ireland)

ABOVE: St. Mary Magdalen, *copy after Bartolome Murillo.*

ABOVE RIGHT: Storm at Sea, (Mid-day), *school of Claude-Joseph Vernet.*

Interior of the Castle Kitchen.

Paintings

Some of the portraits in this room date from the seventeenth century while others are of later date. In the nineteenth century the picture collection at Kilkenny Castle consisted of almost 300 paintings; a mixture of ancestral and royal portraits, Dutch landscapes, Italian religious paintings, and Italianate landscapes. A set of tapestries, part of a series of seven Brussels tapestries – *The Story of Publius Decius Mus a Roman Consul* – attributed to the workshop of Jan Raes, after designs by Sir Peter Paul Rubens (1577-1640), usually hang here but are in conservation.

The Corridor

This nineteenth-century mezzanine corridor was built to house rooms for higher servants; today a range of utilitarian rooms, cloakrooms and other facilities are combined with various staff rooms.

The Kitchen Corridor

Today this corridor houses the Butler Gallery of Contemporary Art and also leads to the Victorian kitchen which, with its old cooking range and rows of polished copper pans, is a good example of its type; it now houses the Castle Bookshop.

THE GARDENS

IN PREVIOUS CENTURIES THE CASTLE was surrounded by parklands and enclosed by gardens with generous tree planting. This was gradually whittled away and changed over the centuries and, when the castle was first handed over to the people of Kilkenny in the 1960s, only fifteen acres of land was attached. However a few years later the Marquess of Ormonde generously donated more land, which has provided a fitting setting for the castle and a splendid amenity area.

The Rose Garden from the terrace steps.

Kilkenny Castle and City from Windgap Hill, 1698 by Francis Place. (National Gallery of Ireland)

After the castle was taken over by the Office of Public Works, new entrances were created to give access to the park. The entrance near the Parade Tower has nineteenth-century cast iron gates that came

originally from Saint Stephen's Green. The open parkland to the south of the castle been replanted with emphasis on trees and shrubs that provide year round colour. Pathways have been restored and some have been extended.

A lead statue of Hermes.

On the west side of the castle a formal garden with axial paths radiating from a central fountain retains much of the basic form that could have been there during the ducal period. The existing fountain is probably the base of an original seventeenth-century water feature. Two lead statues stand on pedestals near the castle: one is of *Hermes* after the original in the Vatican Collection, and the other is of *Diana the Huntress*. All of the garden features, including the terracing, have been recently restored.

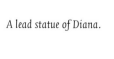

A lead statue of Diana.

PART II

THE BUILDING OF THE CASTLE

The Marshal Castle

The first stone castle, built for William Marshal, 4th Earl of Pembroke (c.1146-1219), was constructed on the site of an earlier timber structure, probably during the first decade of the thirteenth century. Recent excavations have revealed a sod-built structure and sections of a large earthen rampart beneath the garden and parade ranges, both pre-dating the stone building.

The earliest description of the stone castle was recorded in 1307 when the buildings on the site were listed as, 'a castle in which are a hall, four towers, a chapel, a mote (moat) and divers other houses'. This confirms that the form of the castle was similar to that used at the royal castles of Dublin and Limerick in that it was a 'keepless castle'. This meant that it was built without a massive tower (or keep) as its principal feature. Instead it had four towers, an encircling wall, and a moat; within the walls were a hall, chapel and other buildings some of which were probably wooden. Recent excavations have revealed other important facts about the early stone castle. A massive stone base batter, which served as a defensive measure that descended into the dry ditch or moat, has been uncovered on the outer faces of the surviving curtain walls. Two postern gates were also uncovered and have been preserved; one may be seen where it cuts through the well-preserved batter to the right of the entrance gateway. The other is located underneath the floor of the terrace corridor.

A detail from a genealogy of the second Duke of Ormonde.

The Butler Castle

James Butler (c.1360-1405), 3rd Earl of Ormond, purchased Kilkenny Castle in 1391. At the time of that purchase, the setting of Kilkenny Castle was described in documents as 'a great park opposite the gate of the castle there, a dovecot in the same park, a garden, a fishery of the river, a weir there, six acres of land in *le Inches*' and 'castle orchard', 'eleven acres of heye' and 'a garden opposite the gate of the castle'. This additional information places the castle within orchards and meadows, all situated in a park. The gate of the castle at that time faced southwards and was probably of similar structure to the double towered gateway as

The great South Tower, also called the Parade Tower.

illustrated in a later drawing. Features of particular interest from earlier phases of construction are the wicker centering, used to support the vault, which is clearly visible in the lowest level of the west tower and the fine medieval chamber in the Parade (South) Tower that has deep embrasures with defensive arrow loops.

A detail from a genealogy of the second Duke of Ormonde.

The Butler Lordship

James (1390-1452), 4th Earl of Ormond, was a major figure in Ireland where he served as chief governor for long periods. Because of his high status, the fourth earl would have made extensive improvements to his many properties including his castle at Kilkenny. The building of a rectangular tower abutting the circular north tower is possibly from this period. This would have provided more spacious and comfortable lodgings for his family.

TRANSFORMATION

From medieval fortress to renaissance dwelling

During the course of his long life Thomas (1531-1614), 10th Earl of Ormond, began the changes that were to convert the late medieval fortress of Kilkenny Castle into a more modern and comfortable dwelling, though still within the stout encircling walls. Having already transformed Ormond Castle in Carrick on Suir during the 1560s and 70s, in 1580-81 it is recorded that 'This year Thomas Earl of Ormond began the great gallery and the roofing of the Tower over the Nore in the great Castle of Kilkenny'. This would suggest that the Long Gallery, which was situated on the second floor of the central block, was being built at this time and that the roof of the North Tower was raised to that level. A local man, Robert Fraine (Freney or de Freney) is credited with this work. It is also probable that Thomas made improvements to the setting at the castle similar to those at Ormond Castle, where he is known to have extended his gardens and orchards.

A portrait of Thomas Butler (1531-1614), 10th Earl of Ormond by Steven van der Meulen.
(National Gallery of Ireland)

Based on evidence from inventories of the earl's goods we know that the interiors of Kilkenny Castle were lavishly furnished at that time. There would have been priceless Flemish tapestries hanging on the walls, furnishings covered in sumptuous cloth of gold fabric with lace, and embroidered velvet fabrics would have been used on beds, curtains, canopies, cushions, and chairs. Silver bowls, spoons, and damask linens would be used at the table; paintings to decorate the walls, while beds would be dressed with velvet curtains, damask sheets, topped with silk covered quilts.

The great sale

When Thomas died without a legitimate male heir, the bulk of the Ormond properties, including Kilkenny Castle, were taken over by his daughter Elizabeth and her second husband Richard Preston, Lord Dingwall (d.1628). Under their ownership some interiors in the castle were refurbished. New tapestries for the Great Chamber and tawny velvet bed hangings were ordered from London as well as gold and silver fringing 'for beds chairs and stools'. Following the sudden deaths in 1628 of both Elizabeth and her husband there were further complications in the Ormond inheritance and a great sale of the contents of the castle took place in 1630. An inventory taken at that time lists only sixteen chambers within the buildings and describes bare interiors, indicating that at least some of the rooms had been stripped of their contents.

The castle in Cromwellian times

Kilkenny was the focus for the Catholic Confederacy and had suffered badly when under siege by Cromwell's forces in 1650. A detailed survey, carried out between 1654 and 1656, contains valuable information, and describes the castle as having only three towers by this date. The survey also informs us that the 'top of the battlements' were 132 foot long by 20 foot wide and that there were twenty-five rooms in the castle. Also described in the survey were: a hall, a kitchen, an unnamed building and a long, narrow, brick 'house built for soldiers' containing eleven rooms. Outside the castle gate were an 'outergate court' and a huge double 'great stable block'.

Detail from Kilkenny Castle and St. Canice's Cathedral, 1698 by Francis Place. In this drawing the gatehouse of the castle can be clearly seen.
(National Gallery of Ireland)

The 'Magnificent Palace'

During the early 1660s, even though Kilkenny Castle was described as being 'in pretty good repair already', and as 'a pretty house and (with) brave stables', the family's new ducal status meant that not only the castle but other Ormond properties would be remodelled. An extensive programme of building and refurbishment began around 1662, and work continued on the castle while the duke and duchess resided in London between 1669 and 1675.

A seventeenth-century 'armed chair' with embossed leather covering, bought at the Kilkenny Castle Sale in 1935.

When the ducal couple returned from England in 1675, inventory was taken of the contents of the castle. Over one hundred rooms were listed in the various buildings, including the old gatehouse where there was a porter's lodge and a room 'over the gate'. Within the central block of the castle new apartments for the duke and duchess were being created from the earlier old-fashioned interiors, and the State Apartment was renovated. These alterations were in keeping with fashionable, formal planning and symmetrical arrangements then current in European and English great houses. A veritable army of craftsmen was employed at the castle to carry out these changes. Accommodation within the building was provided for stone carvers, painters, gilders, carpenters, upholsterers and various other skilled men. Lavish furnishings were installed in the interiors and hundreds of paintings were hung on the walls of the formal rooms. A reminder of this phase of the building may be seen in the rainwater heads on the drainpipes in the courtyard, (some are later replicas) which bear the date 1682; these may also have been erected to commemorate Ormond's elevation to a dukedom in the English peerage, which occurred in the same year.

Decorated wooden panelling from the Parade Tower in Kilkenny Castle, originally this was painted white with gold leaf gilding.

A detail from decorated wooden panelling from the Parade Tower in Kilkenny Castle.

Detail from a portrait of Elizabeth Preston, Baroness Dingwall and Duchess of Ormond (1615-84) attributed to David des Granges.

A view of Kilkenny Castle from St. John's Bridge 1698, by Francis Place. (National Gallery of Ireland)

The Gardens

At this time the setting of the castle was also transformed. Formal gardens were created with long avenues of trees planted, including oak and ash. Various schemes for at least three fountains were proposed. Other features added to the gardens included an elevated 'leaden' terrace that was constructed in the area where the present Rose Garden is situated. A collection of statuary was ordered, on behalf of Ormond, from John Bonnier the sculptor. The statuary was to be made of 'hard mettle or hardened leaden' and it was to be based on a similar group that stood in the Privy Garden of the Royal Palace of Whitehall. Figures of Diana, the Sabine woman, Hercules, Comodius, and Antonius were to be made full size and mounted on plinths, at a cost of £40 each, also sixteen smaller figures of boys, $2^{1}/_{2}$ feet in height, at £5 each. Orders were also given for designs for 'emblems...to exemplify the 12 signs (of the Zodiac) and 4 seasons'.

A detail from a view of Kilkenny 1698, by Francis Place showing the Banqueting House.

The Banqueting House

To the south-east of the castle a 'water house' was built outside the line of the original castle wall and beside the Bowling Green. This small building contained a summer banqueting chamber, and in terms of design, is probably one of the earliest and most correctly Classical buildings erected in Ireland. It was circular in shape with a peristyle or continuous colonnade. The interior had a black and white paved floor, with a painted ceiling decorated with angels. A fountain stood in the centre of the floor and this was described as 'a Jet d'Eau or throw of water' by Thomas Dineley (d.1695), an English antiquarian who was visiting Kilkenny in 1680. From this small building, water was pumped up to the castle by means of 'an Engine of curious artifice' driven by a horse that was housed in the basement storey.

The Classical Gateway

It was probably during the early 1680s and after Dineley's visit that work commenced on a new Classical gateway that was inserted in the curtain wall. This is the same gateway that today provides the principal entrance to the castle. Sir Hugh May (1622-84) described as a 'virtuoso' sent designs for this project but it seems that he did not want his 'draught' altered because he 'proposed to show ye exact shape and beauty of the Peers' (sic]. There is conflicting evidence about the stone used on the original piers for the gate. One suggestion is that they were of Caen stone that had been shipped from France and brought up river from Inistioge while another commentator describes them as being of Portland stone. There is a detailed correspondence throughout 1681 about the various difficulties raised by the scale of the piers and some of these were referred to Sir Christopher Wren (1632-1723) the architect of Saint Paul's Cathedral in London. Further problems such as the batter of the wall and the amount of masonry that should be taken down were also discussed; in the end the removal of sections measuring 'six foot to each side' was suggested. Construction of this gateway seems to have been intermittent; work continued during the second duke's time, and Sir William Robinson (1643-1712) is usually suggested as having been involved in the building of it, and it may be that the original plans as drawn up by Hugh May were not followed.

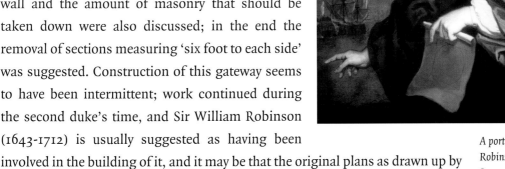

A portrait of Sir William Robinson (1643-1712), Surveyor General and architect by Sir Godfrey Kneller.

(Philip Mould Historical Portraits, London)

Treason

Another James Butler (1665-1745) succeeded his grandfather as second duke of Ormonde in 1688, the same year that a constitutional crisis erupted in England when William of Orange landed in Devon. In the ensuing war Ormonde fought on William's side. In 1689, Kilkenny Castle was taken over by the Jacobite Viscount Galmoy who lodged barrels of powder and shot in the cellar of the

'Round Tower'. The victorious King William was a guest of Ormonde's at Kilkenny Castle before his return to England.

Some alterations were made to the interiors of the castle to suit the needs of the second ducal couple and a new building was begun on the eastern side of the courtyard. Mary Somerset, (1665-1733) 2nd duchess of Ormonde, visited Kilkenny and wrote enthusiastically about her reception there. 'I have been received with as much respect as the greatest woman in the world could have been both by Civil, Military and Ecclesiastical persons'. But, following Ormonde's involvement in a Jacobite plot of 1715, a bill of attainder for treason was passed against him.

In 1717 an inventory was taken of the contents of the castle for appraisal on behalf of the Commissioners of Forfeited Estates. A sale of the goods of the castle was advertised in the Dublin Gazette of 1718, but the extent of this has not been established. By the time inventory was taken for the sale, the interior of the castle was suffering from neglect. The damask hangings of the state bed, which had gold and silver fringing were described as being 'much tarnished'. Decay was widespread and even the curtains on the ducal bed had been 'cut and carried away by thieves'. Ormonde's brother, Charles, Earl of Arran, was permitted by an act of the English Parliament to purchase some of the Irish properties including Kilkenny Castle in 1721 and thus secured ownership of the castle for the family.

A portrait of Mary Somerset, 2nd Duchess of Ormonde (1665-1733) artist unknown.

Eighteenth century decline

A portrait of James Butler, 2nd Duke of Ormonde (1665-1745), artist unknown after Michael Dahl.

There was a hiatus in the Butler family occupation of the castle between Ormonde's exile and the return of his cousins from the Kilcash branch, to the castle. During that time various agents lived there and they reported that the premises were in a 'ruinous state' as early as 1721. Some money was expended for essential repairs in 1722, but twenty-five years later a visitor was comparing the castle's decrepit state to that of 'a weather-beaten ship in a storm, after a long voyage with all her cargo thrown overboard'.

A view of Kilkenny City c. 1757 attributed to Thomas Mitchell, the castle is on the left above the river.
(National Gallery of Ireland)

The Butlers return to Kilkenny Castle

When Walter Butler (1703-83), (de jure) 16th Earl of Ormonde succeeded his cousin John to the depleted estates, he faced a huge task, that of repairing and refurbishing the long neglected buildings. Edward Ledwich leaves us a detailed description of the castle during Walter's tenancy, c.1783, when he informs us that the castle 'has lately been much improved'. He also remarks that 'in the courtyard are the foundations of buildings and opposite the door of the house is a clock placed in an old tower'. The foundations referred to were probably those of the buildings of the second duke, and the clock had been inserted in the medieval gatehouse. Ledwich also informs us that the couple living at the castle 'continued as Roman Catholics' and he goes on to describe their chapel, which had an alter, a tabernacle and 'a Madonna over it'. Another visitor, Philip Luckombe in 1780, also mentions a chapel but situates it outside the gate and tells us that two of the buildings in the courtyard are 'under repair'. He then comments that one is being rebuilt, 'but in a taste too modern for a building of such antiquity, and too frippery for one of such magnitude'.

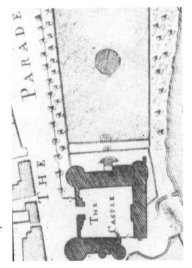

Detail from a map of Kilkenny 1758 by John Rocque showing the plan of the castle when the gate house and north range were still intact.
(the Board of Trinity College Dublin)

33

Family fortunes rise again

Walter Butler (1770-1820), 1st Marquess of Ormonde (2nd creation), who was profligate with his wealth, ran with the fashionable crowd surrounding the Prince Regent. He ordered furniture and fittings from firms in Dublin and London. During an extensive refurbishment that took place at the castle in

Detail from a portrait of Walter Butler (1770-1820), 1st Marquess of Ormonde (2nd creation) painted by Sir William Beechey.

1801-3, prior to the marriage of Walter to an English heiress Anna Maria Price-Clarke, items such as expensive wallpapers were purchased from J. Munns and Company in London; portraits were commissioned from the fashionable London painter Sir William Beechey; and over £7,000 was spent on furniture from suppliers in London and Dublin.

An aerial view of the Stables at Kilkenny Castle attributed to the architect Charles Virpyle.

Building work 1760-1820

Building work carried out at Kilkenny Castle during the period 1760-1820 included fine stables attributed to Charles Virpyle (fl. 1774-1807) and the rebuilding of Butler House, previously the Dower House and now a hotel, which has elegant decorative interior plasterwork. Apart from Luckcombe's reference to a new building, the work on the core buildings at the castle seems to have been fairly superficial and concentrated on the interiors, although it was towards the latter part of this period that demolition of the square tower and other buildings on the east (river side) was carried out. The medieval gatehouse and the remains of the southern curtain wall were also swept away at this time.

The nineteenth-century castle – Castellated Baronial style

The next rebuilding, and perhaps most relevant to the castle we see today, was that which began shortly after 1825. In that year Grace Louisa Staples, (1779-1860) Countess of Ormond, was reportedly walking with the architect William Robertson (1770-1850) when it was noticed that the courtyard wall of the central block of the castle was leaning outwards at a dangerous angle. However, it is probable that this story is apocryphal and that a decision had already been taken to renovate the castle buildings in the then fashionable Castellated Baronial style. Robertson had exhibited architectural designs for the castle in that style at the Royal Academy, some twenty years previously. Such a 'Gothick' remodelling, in common with many other buildings in Ireland, would have been fashionable and also have served as a reminder of the family's long ancestry. William Bartlett, a topographer, made an amusing comment at the time when he described Kilkenny Castle as 'being modernised within and unmodernised without'. The use of the Baronial style by Robertson was not entirely successful, considering the extent of his reconstruction; it was more a superficial application of motifs rather than a robust rebuilding, although it should be said that some of his architectural drawings for Kilkenny show a more coherent approach than was finally utilised. Robertson submitted building accounts for the period 1824-1843 and one such bill 'for the total account of William Robertson' came to £30,815. Huge amounts of money were also spent on the interiors and on refurnishing the house in the newest styles. More paintings were added to the existing collection and others were sent for cleaning and restoration. While the extensive building works were being carried out under Robertson, the family moved, with most of their belongings, across the road to the remodelled and renovated Butler House. They lived there for almost twenty years.

A view of Kilkenny Castle from the College Meadows, by William Robertson. This highly finished drawing may be one of a number showing proposed designs for rebuilding the castle. (The Knight of Glin)

The many changes made to the castle by Robertson included the building of the impressive Picture Gallery on earlier foundations, the replacement of the old roofs on the circular towers where battlements were added, and the insertion of new windows. Various other towers, also crenellated were added. On the courtyard elevation of the central block a *porte-cochère* was built; this was later extended to form the existing glazed entrance corridor.

A detail of the carved stone festoons on the Classical gate that were added during William Robertson's remodelling of the castle.

It was also during this phase of building that the classical entrance gateway was remodelled. Robertson had described the gateway in 1812 as being 'enriched by Corinthian pilasters carrying a pediment, is Roman, and was intended to have been a splendid entrance'. The gateway had remained unfinished since the early eighteenth century and according to Robertson there were 'bosses of Portland stone, probably intended to have been chiselled into swags of drapery and festoons of flowers'. His early designs show a castellated style of gateway but these were not used, instead the Corinthian capitals and pediment were retained, while the swags and festoons that were added complement the classical style.

The architectural input of Deane & Woodward

Ultimately, Robertson's designs failed to please the Ormondes and his buildings also had intrinsic flaws, such as the flat roofs that leaked, on the gallery block and elsewhere. In order to remedy some of the defects, a prominent firm of architects, Deane and Woodward, was called in by Frances Jane Paget (1817-1903), Marchioness of Ormonde, during the 1860s to re-roof the castle, remodel the Picture Gallery range, and make further alterations to the garden elevation of the central block. This firm of architects had submitted lavish designs in a French Chateau style for the gallery however these were turned down in favour of more limited alterations to Robertson's building. These alterations addressed the problem of the Picture Gallery by installing a new pitched roof with glazed central area. Oriel windows on the courtyard elevation were inserted, and the tracery in the gable window was altered to an Early English style. Within the gallery the open roof was decorated by John Hungerford Pollen (1820-1902) in a mixture of styles ranging from pre-Raphaelite to interlace with gilded animal and bird heads on the cross beams.

A detail of the Picture Gallery showing the triple lancet window that was inserted during the Deane and Woodward work on William Robertson's picture gallery.

Also designed by Pollen, the massive double fireplace in Carrara marble was decorated with scenes from the history of the Ormonde family; the decoration is attributed to Charles Harrison, but it was supplied by the firm of Ballantyne, Chimneypiece Manufacturers of Dorset Street Dublin. A 'Moorish' staircase enclosing a winter garden with delightful carved stone details on the cut stone arcade, also by Harrison, was added in order to provide a direct and impressive access to the remodelled gallery. Venetian Gothic windows were added to the garden elevation of the central block, some with cusped arches flanked by slim marble shafts and balconies, while the doorway leading to the Rose Garden was also remodelled.

A small gasworks was built in the grounds of the castle. This fuel was used to heat the castle and also for lighting by gasoliers.

The final result of these building campaigns was the mixture of styles we see today. Robertson's muscular Castellated Baronial contrasts with the lighter Venetian Gothic motifs that sit somewhat incongruously with the essentially medieval appearance of the original castle.

The Butlers depart from Kilkenny Castle

The Deane and Woodward works were to be the last major rebuilding at Kilkenny Castle until a series of phased building and conservation programmes were carried out by State agencies from the 1970s onwards. The Butler family had moved out and auctioned the contents of the castle in 1935. There followed years of neglect and dereliction. Throughout the 1940s and 50s various proposals were put forward about the future of the castle but it was not until Mr. C.J. Lytle made a generous gift of £20,000 towards restoration work that any serious intent could be followed up. When the castle was formally taken over by the State in 1969, the Office of Public Works had agreed to assume responsibility for the restoration of

The garden front of Kilkenny Castle showing the Venetian Gothic windows with small balconies that were inserted during the Deane and Woodward work on the castle.

the gardens and open parklands, and the Picture Gallery wing was renovated and reopened during the 1970s. Later, the central block and North Tower were investigated, when the principal problem was found to be dry and wet rot, which had attacked the timber structures within the walls of the castle. The fungus had spread throughout the building rotting floors, roof timbers, wall panelling, doors, windows and other joinery so that extensive reconstruction of the interiors was the only option available to the architects involved. However, before beginning another building campaign an archaeological investigation was carried out. The information gathered at that time has greatly increased our understanding of the origins and development of the castle.

The interior of the central block was virtually rebuilt but, where possible, original building materials that had been salvaged were reused. In areas where these had deteriorated or were missing, faithful reproductions of high quality were used for features such as decorative plasterwork cornices and suchlike. Great care was also taken with other interior fittings. Copies were created from original pelmets, wall coverings, carpets, and bookcases in the library. The overall intention was to recreate interiors for the Picture Gallery wing and central block based on mid nineteenth-century styles that prevailed when the last Ormonde building campaign at the castle had taken place. A later phase of restoration work has been carried out in the Parade Wing, which includes the two circular towers and the area behind the Classical gateway. It is now used as a conference venue that also serves as a showcase for the imaginative adaptation of a medieval space.

Kilkenny Castle today

Today Kilkenny Castle stands as an example of several phases of development in Irish architectural styles ranging from the stone built, moated Norman fortress on a commanding site through later styles incorporated in the buildings, including the impressive seventeenth-century Classical gateway. The eighteenth century saw the building of the elegant, crescent shaped stables and the nineteenth-century rebuilding and remodelling introduced the Castellated Baronial style with additional Ruskinian Gothic motifs. The final phase of the latest conservation and rebuilding process carried out by architects of the Office of Public Works is evident in the modern conference centre housed within the medieval fabric of the Parade Tower.

The interior of the Parade (South) Tower showing the modern conference centre facilities that have been installed there.

PART III

LORDS OF THE CASTLE

The Marshals

William Marshal (c.1146-1219), called the Marshal and 4th Earl of Pembroke, soldier and administrator, was born a younger son who had risen through the ranks of the Norman hierarchy because of his prowess as a soldier, skill as a courtier, and success in knightly tournaments. An advantageous marriage in 1189 to the heiress Isabel de Clare (c.1171-1220), daughter of Richard fitz Gilbert de Clare known as Strongbow and his wife Aoife Mac Murchada, enabled Marshal to join an elite group that held great swathes of lands in Wales, Ireland and also in Normandy. A notable soldier, he had travelled extensively in Europe going east as far as the Kingdom of Jerusalem. Before his marriage and during the 1180s Marshal served in the royal household where he began to accumulate wealth. On the death of his elder brother, Marshal had inherited the family's lands and, when King John came to the throne 1199, he was finally granted the lands and title of earl of Pembroke.

A detail from a genealogy of the second Duke of Ormonde.

In the process of extending their feudal lordships in Ireland the Marshals had, over just two generations, greatly influenced the future shape of Leinster. During that time they built castles, brought in settlers, founded boroughs, and endowed religious houses. When Marshal went to claim his Pembrokeshire lands in 1201 he crossed over to his lands in Leinster. In 1207, having fallen out of favour with the king, he retired to Ireland with his military household in attendance. He remained here for a period of six years, with just two brief visits across the Irish Sea when summoned by King John. During that time he organised his Irish estates and it is likely that he was also building at Kilkenny. When he departed from Ireland, his wife Isabel de Clare, who was also a great magnate in her own right, took charge of his estates.

The second generation

On Isabel's death in 1220, just one year after her husband, her estates in Ireland passed to their eldest son William (c.1190-1231), 5th Earl of Pembroke, who also rose to be a great magnate. William was appointed Justiciar of Ireland in 1224 for a term of two years. He was reputed to be a notable builder of castles and was responsible for much of the structure of the great castle of Chepstow in Wales.

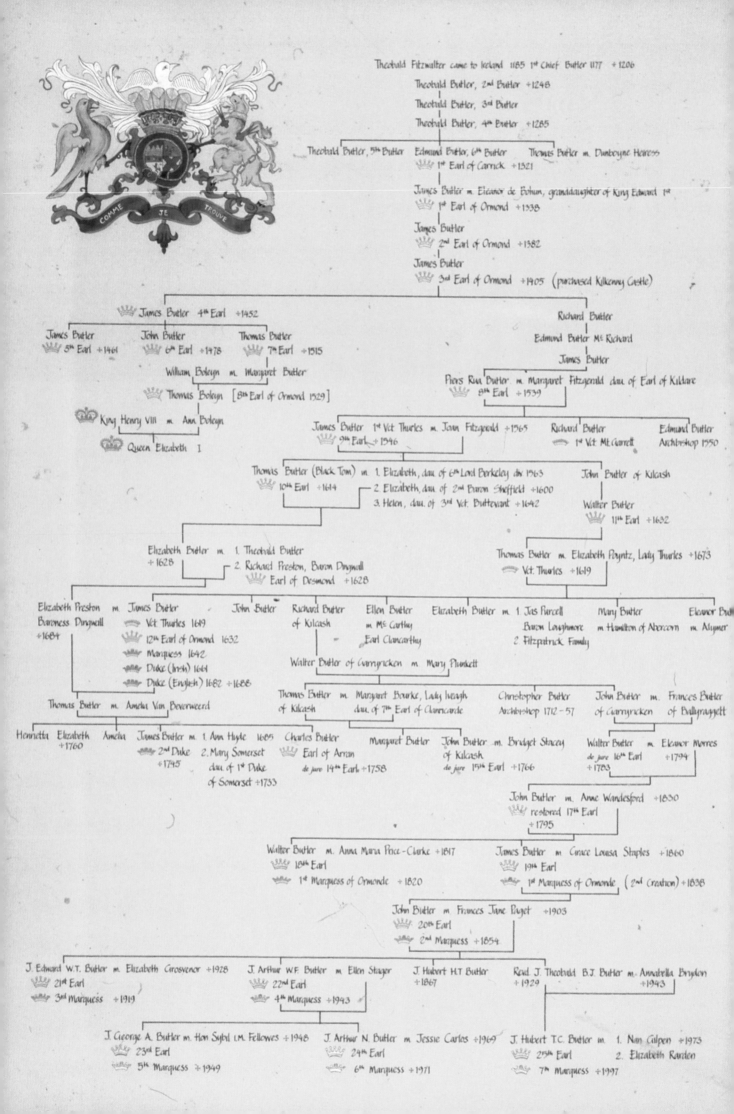

COMME JE TROUVE

Theobald Fitzwalter came to Ireland 1185 1st Chief Butler 1177 +1206
Theobald Butler, 2nd Butler +1248
Theobald Butler, 3rd Butler
Theobald Butler, 4th Butler +1285

Theobald Butler, 5th Butler — Edmund Butler, 6th Butler 1st Earl of Carrick +1321 — Thomas Butler m. Dunboyne Heiress

James Butler m. Eleanor de Bohun, granddaughter of King Edward 1st 1st Earl of Ormond +1338

James Butler 2nd Earl of Ormond +1382

James Butler 3rd Earl of Ormond +1405 (purchased Kilkenny Castle)

James Butler 4th Earl +1452 — Richard Butler

James Butler 5th Earl +1461 — John Butler 6th Earl +1478 — Thomas Butler 7th Earl +1515 — Edmund Butler Mc Richard — James Butler

William Boleyn m. Margaret Butler — Piers Rua Butler m. Margaret Fitzgerald dau. of Earl of Kildare 8th Earl +1539

Thomas Boleyn [8th Earl of Ormond 1529]

King Henry VIII m. Ann Boleyn — James Butler 1st Vct. Thurles m. Joan Fitzgerald +1565 9th Earl +1546 — Richard Butler 1st Vct. Mt. Garrett — Edmund Butler Archbishop 1550

Queen Elizabeth 1

Thomas Butler (Black Tom) m. 1. Elizabeth, dau. of 6th Lord Berkeley div. 1563 10th Earl +1614 — 2. Elizabeth, dau. of 2nd Baron Sheffield +1600 — 3. Helen, dau. of 3rd Vct. Buttevant +1642 — John Butler of Kilcash

Walter Butler 11th Earl +1632

Elizabeth Butler m. 1. Theobald Butler +1628 — 2. Richard Preston, Baron Dingwall Earl of Desmond +1628 — Thomas Butler m. Elizabeth Poyntz, Lady Thurles +1673 Vct. Thurles +1619

Elizabeth Preston Baroness Dingwall +1684 m. James Butler Vct. Thurles 1619, 12th Earl of Ormond 1632, Marquess 1642, Duke (Irish) 1661, Duke (English) 1682 +1688 — John Butler — Richard Butler of Kilcash — Ellen Butler m. Mc Carthy Earl Clancarthy — Elizabeth Butler m. 1. Jas Purcell Baron Loughmore 2. Fitzpatrick Family — Mary Butler m. Hamilton of Abercorn — Eleanor Butler m. Alymer

Walter Butler of Garryricken m. Mary Plunkett

Thomas Butler m. Amelia Van Beverweerd — Thomas Butler of Kilcash m. Margaret Bourke, Lady Iveagh dau. of 7th Earl of Clanricarde — Christopher Butler Archbishop 1712-57 — John Butler m. Frances Butler of Garryricken of Ballyraggett

Henrietta Elizabeth +1760 — Amelia — James Butler m. 1. Ann Hyde 1685 2nd Duke +1745 2. Mary Somerset dau. of 1st Duke of Somerset +1733 — Charles Butler Earl of Arran de jure 14th Earl +1758 — Margaret Butler — John Butler m. Bridget Stacey of Kilcash de jure 15th Earl +1766 — Walter Butler m. Eleanor Morres de jure 16th Earl +1783 +1794

John Butler m. Anne Wandesford +1830 restored 17th Earl +1795

Walter Butler m. Anna Maria Price-Clarke +1817 18th Earl 1st Marquess of Ormonde +1820 — James Butler m. Grace Louisa Staples +1860 19th Earl 1st Marquess of Ormonde (2nd Creation) +1838

John Butler m. Frances Jane Paget +1903 20th Earl 2nd Marquess +1854

J. Edward W.T. Butler m. Elizabeth Grosvenor +1928 21st Earl 3rd Marquess +1919 — J. Arthur W.F. Butler m. Ellen Stager 22nd Earl 4th Marquess +1943 — J. Hubert H.T. Butler +1867 — Revd. J. Theobald B.J. Butler m. Annabella Brydon +1929 +1943

J. George A. Butler m. Hon Sybil L.M. Fellowes +1948 23rd Earl 5th Marquess +1949 — J. Arthur N. Butler m. Jessie Carlos +1969 24th Earl 6th Marquess +1971 — J. Hubert T.C. Butler m. 1. Nan Gilpen +1973 25th Earl 7th Marquess +1997 2. Elizabeth Rardon

He died suddenly in 1231 and was succeeded by his brother Richard, who is recorded as dying in his castle at Kilkenny after wounds received at a battle on the Curragh, County Kildare. Following the death of the fifth and last Marshal son, Anslem in 1245, their inheritance was eventually divided between representatives of their five sisters who were co-heiresses.

The Walters arrive in Ireland

The first ancestor of the Butler family to come to Ireland was Theobald Walter (d.1205). Of Norman origin, his father held lands in Weeton, Lancashire, England. Well connected through their mother, Matilda, co-heir of the Lord of Parham, Suffolk, Theobald and his brother Hubert, who was later Archbishop of Canterbury and Justiciar of England, moved in the higher echelons of Norman society. While the brothers were being raised in the household of Ranulf de Glanville, Justiciar of England during the 1180s, Prince John, son of Henry II, was also attached there. Theobald accompanied John when the prince came to Ireland in 1185 to assume his lordship of the country. Like many other Norman magnates, Theobald established religious houses at Arklow in Wicklow, Owney in Limerick, and Nenagh in Tipperary. When Theobald died he had extensive land holdings in Munster and south Leinster.

LEFT: A family tree of the Butlers.

The Butlers of Ormond(e)[1]

The derivation of the name Butler of Ormond is complicated. Originally the family surname was Walter. It was during the reign of Henry II, while Theobald Walter was styled *pincerna* (Latin) or *boteillier* (Norman French) 'butler', or ceremonial cup-bearer to Prince John, Lord of Ireland, that the surname Butler came into usage. Theobald was also granted large tracts of lands in Ireland by Prince John and it was from the situation of some of these grants that the later title Oir Mhumhan (Gaelic) – East Munster or Ormond – derives.

The fourteenth century Butlers, created earls of Ormond, and the acquisition of Kilkenny Castle

When James Butler (c.1305-1338) was created the first earl of Ormond in 1328 he was also granted a life-grant of the liberty of Tipperary, which became the Butler Palatinate in that area that was held by his descendants until 1716. It was another James (c.1360-1405), 3rd Earl of Ormond, magnate and Justiciar of Ireland, who acquired Kilkenny Castle and added strategic lands in the Barrow-Nore-Suir

---

1 The spelling of the earldom of Ormond until the eighteenth century was without an e, and as the first duke usually signed himself Ormond, this usage has been retained to differentiate him from his grandson and those who followed. In referring to the family as an entity before 1688, Ormond is used, and thereafter Ormonde.

basin to their already extensive holdings. Under his personal rule the Butler lordship became a more cohesive entity. Nearby Gowran was where the family's main residence was situated and it was there also that the early earls were buried.

At the time of his first visit to Ireland in 1394-95, King Richard II regarded Ormond as the premier Irish earl and appointed him Justiciar of Ireland. By this time the Ormonds had forged a network of alliances with both the Irish and Gaelicised Anglo-Normans, and had now reached a position where they were in possession of one of the three most powerful Anglo-Norman lordships in Ireland.

The Butler Lordship in the fifteenth century

James (1390-1452), 4th Earl of Ormond, also a magnate and administrator, was a major figure in Ireland where he served as chief governor for long periods. The fourth earl's three sons by his first marriage succeeded him as earls of Ormond, although their interests were engaged mainly in England where a bitter civil war (the Wars of the Roses) was in progress. James (1420-61), 5th Earl of Ormond, succeeded his father and lived out his life in England where he was also created earl of Wiltshire. The fifth earl was executed in 1461 for his part in the civil war there. His two brothers – John (d.1478), who also died in England and Thomas (d.1515), who was reputed to be 'one of the richest subjects in the Kingdom' – succeeded him.

The sixteenth-century crisis in the Ormond succession

Two outstanding members of the Butler family emerge during the sixteenth century. These were Piers Butler (d.1539), 8th Earl of Ormond and Earl of Ossory, and his grandson, Thomas Butler (1532-1614), 10th Earl of Ormond. Piers was cousin to the previous earls of Ormond and during their prolonged absence from Ireland, his father Sir James Butler (d.1487) had laid claim to the Ormond land and titles. This had precipitated a crisis in the Ormond succession when the seventh earl had died without an heir. One of the heirs general to the Ormond inheritance was Thomas Boleyn, whose mother was a Butler. Boleyn was the father of Anne, whose star was rising at the court of Henry VIII. As a consequence of the king's favour, Thomas was successful in obtaining the titles of Ormond and Wiltshire.

Meanwhile, Piers had seized Kilkenny Castle (c.1498) and with his wife, Margaret fitzGerald (d.1542), the dynamic daughter of the earl of Kildare, probably improved the living accommodation there. After a prolonged struggle, eventually aided by Henry VIII's Chancellor, Cardinal Thomas Wolsey, Piers was granted the earldom of Ossory and was finally successful in regaining the Ormond title in 1538. This title was inherited by his son James, 9th Earl of Ormond and Earl of Ossory.

Thomas, 10th Earl of Ormond and Earl of Ossory

Piers grandson, Thomas (1531-1614), also inherited these titles. Thomas was the eldest of seven sons of James, the ninth earl, who had died prematurely just four years after coming into his inheritance. Like his father, Thomas had spent much of his youth at court in England. He was to become one of the most powerful figures in Irish politics of the period, holding several high offices of State and continuing to serve the Queen. Thomas had been married, firstly to Elizabeth Berkley (d.1582), and secondly Elizabeth Sheffield (d. 1600), but was still without a legitimate male heir when, in 1601, he took a third wife, Helen Barry (d. 1640). Thomas's only son-in-law, Theobald, Viscount Thurles, was designated as heir, but predeceased him in 1613. This was to lead to another round of serious complications in the Ormond inheritance.

Detail from a portrait of Thomas Butler (1531-1614), 10th Earl of Ormond by Steven van der Meulen.
(National Gallery of Ireland)

The seventeenth-century

It was during this century that the Ormonds reached the apogee of power, position, and estates. The long drawn out dispute over the Ormond inheritance had ended with an arranged marriage between Elizabeth Preston (1615-84), granddaughter of Thomas, the tenth earl, and her cousin James Butler (1610-88) 12th Earl of Ormond, later 1st Marquess and 1st Duke of Ormond. Ormond, as a loyal supporter of the beleaguered King Charles I, had been made commander-in-chief of the king's forces in Ireland in 1641. Following the royalists' defeat at the hands of the Cromwellian army, Ormond crossed to France and spent another decade travelling about Northern Europe with the exiled king, Charles II. After the restoration of Charles II to the throne of England, Ormond was elevated to a dukedom for his loyal service to the Stuart monarchy. As Ireland's sole duke and Viceroy, Ormond had reached the pinnacle of aristocratic society in the country.

Detail from a portrait of James Butler (1610-88), 12th earl and 1st duke of Ormonde attributed to John Michael Wright.

When another James Butler (1665-1745) succeeded his grandfather as second duke of Ormonde, he came into a vast inheritance from both of his grandparents. Ormonde, having

Charles Butler (1671-1758), 2nd Earl of Arran, attributed to Hans Hysing.

RIGHT: Detail from a portrait of Walter Butler (1703-83), de jure 16th Earl of Ormonde, by Robert Hunter.

A portrait of Grace Louisa Staples (1779-1860), Marchioness of Ormonde by John Sauders.

allied himself with the victorious King William in the constitutional crisis that beset England in 1688, enjoyed an amicable relationship and prospered under the king and his successor Queen Anne. However he began to drift towards the Jacobites and, shortly after the accession of Hanovarian George I in 1716, Ormonde was impeached. He went into exile, leaving his wife in London, eventually to live out his days in Avignon, France. As a consequence the Ormonde properties were seized. The English estates were sold but Ormonde's brother Charles (1671 -1758), Earl of Arran, was successful in saving Kilkenny Castle and other properties that formed the Irish part of the Ormonde inheritance.

The eighteenth century

It was not until the 1760s that Walter Butler (1703-83), (de jure) 16th Earl of Ormonde succeeded his father John Butler of Kilcash and moved into the castle. In turn his son, another John Butler (d.1795) inherited and, having converted to the Protestant faith, was confirmed as (de facto) earl of Ormonde in 1791. John made an advantageous marriage to a Wandesford heiress and the family fortunes were on the rise again. This was particularly evident when John's son, another Walter (1770-1820), 1st Marquess of Ormonde (2nd creation), succeeded to the

title and property. In 1799 the Irish estates of the Ormondes were worth £22,000 a year. The Crown also paid compensation of £216,000 to Walter when he sold the Butler's hereditary prisage of wines which they held for centuries.

The nineteenth century

James Butler (1774-1838), 1st Marquess of Ormonde (3rd creation), and his wife Grace Louisa Staples (1779-1860), were responsible for a major programme of building works on the castle. During that time the family moved to live in Butler House, the Dower house on

Patrick Street, Kilkenny. Their son John Butler (1808-54), 2nd Marquess of Ormonde, was a great traveller and kept journals of his travels around Europe. He was also deeply interested in collecting art, and during his ownership the Picture Gallery was built and many new paintings were acquired. It was John's wife, Frances Jane Paget (1817-1903), who brought in the architects Deane and Woodward to make further alterations to the castle buildings. The last marquess of Ormonde to live at Kilkenny Castle was James Edward Butler (1844-1919), 3rd Marquess of Ormonde, who, with his wife Elizabeth Harriet

A portrait of John Butler (1808-54), 2nd Marquess of Ormonde (3rd creation), by Henry Weigall, Jnr.

Grosvenor (1856-1928), entertained British royalty at the castle in a final aristocratic episode. It was a way of life that, by the beginning of the twentieth century, had become an anachronism. Forthcoming changes in land tenure, as

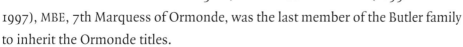

well as in the social and political climate, were to bring the era of the great landed estates in Ireland to a close.

A portrait Harriet Elizabeth Grosvenor (1856-1928), Marchioness of Ormonde by Hon. Henry Richard Graves.

The twentieth century

In 1935 the contents of the castle were put up for sale that lasted over a period of ten days. The castle buildings deteriorated during a period of neglect until 1967 when James Arthur Butler (1893-1971), 6th Marquess of Ormonde, generously presented Kilkenny Castle to members of the Kilkenny Castle Restoration Committee for a sum of £50. James Hubert Butler (1899-1997), MBE, 7th Marquess of Ormonde, was the last member of the Butler family to inherit the Ormonde titles.

James Arthur Butler (1893-1971), 6th Marquess of Ormonde.